Formation Football

Formation Football

How football shapes us

By

Rodney, Todd, and Kelly Drury.

Published by Redneck Mystic Media

Published by Redneck Mystic Media
3011 N. Delaware St.
Peoria IL 61603

ISBN 978-1-942421-12-2

Contents

Listening

"How do you WIN? By getting average players to play good and good players to play great. That's how you WIN."--Bum Phillips

Communicating can be tricky at any time, but when a person is exhausted, communicating can be nearly impossible. That is what must happen in a football game. Clean and concise information needs to be communicated to exhausted and distracted players.

From the play call to the snap count and from the audible to the time out, football demands great communication in a timely fashion.

Football Formation

I have been in more than one situation where one coach was trying to get us to run a play and another coach was trying to call a time out. The quarterback was trying to get us huddled up and the guy bringing in the play was turning around and running back off the field as the play caller changed things. The guy next to me started complaining, and someone else told him to shut up. Heavy breathing and a half-chewed mouthpiece choked out a list of numbers, and a clap of hands sent you to the line guessing what to do.

What you wanted to happen was a clearly understood play with a sharp focus. Confidence in what to do and how to do it allows you to explode with intention. Instruction aids precision. The ability to hear and listen is essential.

I was like a lot of kids who played both ways in high school. I can recall a time when I was sucking all the oxygen out of the mile-high air in Rapid City. I kept playing but I wasn't a part of the team. My ears were full of my own exhaustion. My focus was on catching my breath when the ball was snapped. Trying to convince the coach that anyone could do a better job than me right then didn't seem like an option. I just wanted out of the game. Others thought I could give more. I just wanted to give up.

Many times, life is like that. We just want out of this job, this marriage, this situation. We stop listening, and relationships and performance falls apart. We have long been working diligently at our job, doing our part, but we are getting tired as the game goes on. The voices that once brought clarity and direction become muddled. We face each day or situation with uncertainty. We just want to stop because listening is hard and tiring work. We are out of breath.

Both football and life have timeouts for a reason. Often a "time out" is about conversation. At other times it is just to catch our breath. If you have timeouts available, use them.

Stop what is happening so that you can make something else happen. Listen. Don't just converse; seek to understand what others are saying. They may not have words, so you might need to be aware of body language, emotions, and attitudes.

Listening doesn't mean we are influenced by all the noise, or advice around us. It means we are submitting ourselves to the control of others. Listening is being receptive to what is necessary even when we are exhausted.

Football Formation

Just remember, if you can't breathe, you probably can't listen.

Destiny

"It's the name on the FRONT of the jersey that matters most, not the one on the BACK."--Joe Paterno, <u>Penn State</u>

In the fall of 1977, I stepped onto the college practice field among a mass of strangers all competing to make the team. Making the team was the first goal. Becoming a starter was the next. In those few days, it was necessary for me to figure out the coaches, get along with a new roommate, become part of a squad and start embracing a new team culture. While all this was going on, what I didn't know was that I was also laying the foundation for lifelong friends, opening my life to trust on new levels, and breaking down stereotypes held by this redneck mystic from South Dakota.

My first encounter of significance that year was with Coach Paul Costa. Paul was a big man and seemed friendly enough, although I think he enjoyed people not knowing that. His ways were direct and intentional, which I liked. I always knew where I stood with Paul and that gave me confidence. When Paul was messing with me, it wasn't about performance or position, it was just the way Paul enjoyed relationships.

Coach Paul was not a peaceful man, but I didn't mind that. I understood the workings of an aggressive man better than one of peace. In no way was Paul cruel, but his nature was not tender by any means. In the mindset of the cowboy country I came from, Paul was all man.

Just as guns have triggers, so did the men I grew up around. Men who went off when you touched the wrong part. Safety with both guns and men with triggers are determined by how you treat them. Respect is required. I respected Paul. I knew he was the kind of man who could go off. While I never was afraid of him, I was aware of his power.

Evangel University didn't choose me. I chose it. My twin brother and I had decided that we would not attend the same college, because we had been competing with one another since pre-birth. We thought it was time to stop. Rick went to Clemson in South Carolina and I leaned toward Nebraska, but I felt that I needed to make a course change in my life. I felt that going to Nebraska would not allow me that change. I just didn't have the character for it. Evangel was my choice.

Walking out of the locker room and into the hallway where we were receiving our practice gear, I met Paul for the first time. He reached down and grabbed the red jersey from my pile of gear and gave me a white one. I didn't know it at the time, but I had just been moved from the defensive to the offensive line. Later, during our first practice I heard the defensive coach calling off names.

Paul saw that I was getting ready to get up from our stretch and run over to my squad. He came over and ripped my name tag off my helmet. He lifted his size twenty finger over his lips to make the "silent" sign and waved his hand in a motion that let me know I was to get back to my stretching. It was a done deal. I had just transitioned from linebacker to lineman.

Football Formation

Not every decision forced upon us in football or in life is a good one. However, that day was a good one. It was good because I enjoyed my coach. Over the next few years we grew to understand each other. I learned much from Paul, I learned about technique, about kindness, about persistence... and about pulling that trigger of his.

At any given moment in life, it might be hard to see what the result will be. Some people believe in fate. Some believe that life is simply a result of our own choices.

I believe the journey into destiny involves some things we choose, and some things that are chosen for us. Thanks, Paul, for choosing me.

Bus Trips

"If you're not gonna go ALL the way, why go at ALL?"--Joe Namath, New York Jets

I once heard that the word fellowship comes from the two words "fellows" and "ship." The idea was of being trapped on a ship together. Maybe relationships mean how we relate to one another while on a ship. Do we have a word to describe what is like to be stuck on a bus trying to relate? Maybe pandemonium could become bus-emonium?

Forty large personalities wedged into average size seats with one bathroom is sometimes too much. Going to the game is usually fine. The focus of the game has a unifying effect. Returning home with ice packs, differing styles of celebration, remorse, and fatigue is another matter. What I enjoyed with anticipation, I could barely tolerate when I wanted to be alone.

Before I formally knew about the concept of personal space, I experienced it. I am contemplative. I don't mind being by myself. On a bus, you are never by yourself. The other players may think that you are like them. They may think you want to talk, to laugh, to fool around, to help them catch up on homework. Some go as far as seeking to organize the entire bus in whatever song, story or joke they are dramatizing. These outgoing types have no clue that others are not being entertained nor encouraged.

Whether you are talking about guys stuck on a ship together for a year or guys stuck on a bus for a thousand miles, fellowship and friendship both have the ship part. Which is a limited amount space with no change of getting off.

Learning how to coexist on a bus full of people not like you is one part of team development. Let me stress. This is a learned behavior. Even those people-people, struggle when they feel the urge to connect with forty others at the same time. Bus-emonium is something we all need to learn.

I am sure a correlation exists between how well we travel together and how well we play as a team. Our ability to solve problems and deal with situations on the bus overflows to problem solving and adversity on the playing field.

I remember one away game when the bus had mechanical issues. Bad directions (pre GPS days) also added to the delay and we were running two hours late. Finally, the coaches pulled over and began grabbing equipment bags from under the bus. We started dressing on the bus. It was the only way we would have time to warm up.

Some guys didn't want to deal with this. Some just did what they were told. Still others added to a bad situation by grumbling and complaining. Everyone wanted a drink. Most of us had to pee. Wedged into a bus seat next to another fully-grown man is tight enough, but add all the gear, the need to pee and being thirsty, and it is YUCK, to the extreme.

What do you do? Do you sing Kumbaya? Do you turn on mood music? Do you yell at everyone to suck it up? Do you just throw up your hands and resign yourself to the turmoil? Yep, all that is going to happen. But what should happen?

Football Formation

In a time like that, all you can do is control yourself, for you can't control others. So that is what you do. Control yourself. Coaches and team leaders try to help this become a reality. Circumstances are un-controllable. But people have a choice.

When life falls apart, when conflict erupts, when there is not a simple answer and no place to hide from the circumstances, what can we do? Control ourselves.

Self-control is a virtue of every successful athlete-and every good bus driver.

Vomit

Football is unconditional love.

-Tom Brady

During my junior year in High School, we had a kid who always got nervous before games. Our team played at the School of Mines and Technology, a twelve-minute bus ride from our high school to their field. After the first trip, we gave Kevin a trash can, because on the first trip, he just puked on the floor of the bus.

Nothing says "Rah, Rah" like a guy puking. The smell is certainly a distraction. Slipping and sliding as we got off the bus clearly led to negative judgments and belittling remarks toward the "vomitee."

I had not considered the role vomit plays in the development of a man. But it does. It prepares him to be a faithful friend and a loving dad. Vomit is a test of character and our gag reflex. Vomit will challenge your pride and see if you are anywhere near a servant leader.

In many ways, everything that comes out of a guy's mouth has impact on those around him. I have heard it said that from out of the heart the mouth speaks. I know for sure that from out of a nervous stomach the mouth projects puke.

Kelly Drury

Sacrifices Made

"Work isn't WORK unless you would rather be DOING something else,"--Don Shula, Miami Dolphins

It is August and I am eight months pregnant with our second child. My husband is involved with someone else, football.

For the last decade, I have supported my husband and his coaching career. It is not something he wanted me to do. It is something <u>we</u> wanted to do. We chose to be a team. Or at least we thought we did.

Football Formation

Team mom holds one child and tries to avoid swelling as the second grows within me. The couch provides some comfort. But I miss my teammate. He's at practice. And if things don't go exactly right, he will be out of state when his next daughter is born.

Hormones may be influencing me here. But I don't want to think about those women who have an even harder time sending their husbands off to work. I don't know how those in the military, police force or even on oil drilling platforms do it. I know I get tired of putting his dinner in the microwave. I didn't sign up to be a single mom. We miss daddy.

Coaching is a full time, never ending job. There is always something more to do or something to do better. Like last week when he was home after the game. There were two hours of video that were digested along with a few pizzas and chips so he could answer the question, "what went wrong?" The truth is, I told him what went wrong in about five minutes; it just took him two hours to figure out I was right.

We share the sacrifice. We share the pain of losing and the time away from family. It is not just his job, it is our lives. There are families who sacrifice more. Some do it differently. But every coach's family does it.

Last week our two-year-old daughter stood looking out the window. One moment she would whisper, "I miss Coach." The next she would say, "I miss Daddy." When we talk about the players, she calls them "my people." Her family of origin is a football team. Daddy and Coach are two words for the same man.

But back to me. I'm a little grumpy, bloated, pregnant, hormonal, emotional and did I say, "ready to have this kid?" Right now, life as a coach's wife is hard. If he is gone on a road trip when I have this child, it might be unbearable for someone. But today I find peace in sharing my husband. I fight the desire to be selfish with the hope that the men developed under his coaching will be better fathers, dads, and men. Even while I complain at times about what I am giving up, I am glad for what this world is gaining.

Last night when he sneaked in bed next to me I gave him a little kiss and said, "Hi Coach." Then I asked him to get dressed and run to the store. I wanted some chocolate.

Football Formation

We Don't Know What We Don't Know

"The thing about football - the important thing about football - is that it is not just about football."
— *Terry Pratchett, Unseen Academicals*

I didn't even know that I didn't know….

- How to live in a dorm
- How to play football and go to college
- How to behave around men
- How to be responsible

I jumped out of my Dodge Superbee, shoved the last bit of French fries in my mouth and started looking for a place to check in. I arrived at college to play football. I was full of excitement. But I had no clue how much I did not know. As I stood at the threshold of my next adventure. I just finished a learning experience. That one changed my life and so would this one.

"Tiny" a six foot seven, three hundred forty-pound construction worker discovered that I was a state champion wrestler and wanted to wrestle for pay checks.

My enlightenment began with concrete, rebar and fire. I was a laborer pushing a Georgia buggy, an oversized wheel barrel that carried up to 400 lbs. of concrete. We were building a stack for a concrete plant. A stack is that concrete tube that sticks up in the air so that whatever was being burned does not pollute the immediate area.

To build the stack you must use a slip form, a platform that lifts itself higher and higher, using the supports you just made. The ironworkers tie rebar inside the form, the laborers pour in concrete, and finishers hang below the platform and smooth it out, 24/7 until the job is completed. Our job took several weeks.

On the third week, as I was backing down the ramp with my load of concrete, the buggy got away from me and it shoved me back into a stack of rebar. One pile of rebar hit me in the back of the neck. Another caught me below my butt and the Georgia buggy's handle shoved me between the two.

Have you ever taken something and smacked a spider against the wall? I was the spider and the "something" was 400 lbs. of concrete trying to suck the life out of me.

But what I didn't know was that those iron workers, who made fun of me, who belittled me for eating peanut butter sandwiches, who got the crane operator to dangle the port-a-potty over my head and shake out some of its contents, had no hesitation to save me.

As I was passing out, I heard the sizzle and pop of gas torches being lit and that unique sound of iron being cut. In moments, the hundreds of bars that pined me were severed and I plopped to the deck. I didn't know that I didn't know men who pick on you will save your life.

When I showed up to play football, I didn't know is wasn't all about football. I didn't know that playing football would change my life, my character and my destiny. Most who came didn't know the power of one man to mold another. We

Football Formation

didn't know how brotherhood, loyalty and lifelong friendships were established.

But now we know.

Bubba

"Losing doesn't make me want to quit, it makes me want to FIGHT that much HARDER"--Bear Bryant, University of Alabama

My first year of college football was also the first year that my school had a football program. I entered like most kids, assuming that everything was in place, ready to go.

The men who came to start that program had walked the life of football for a while. Most of them were from the top. They were National Football League and World football League players who gave of themselves to start something new.

Football Formation

I don't really know what it was like for them to start from scratch, but I can use my imagination. I imagine that it was like homemade ice cream compared to ice cream from Cold Stone. In the end, both are sweet. But the equipment, technology, infrastructure, and resources are vastly different. It was sitting on a kitchen chair turning a handle on a bucket kind of ice cream making.

The pre-season and whole season was a list of "first time everything." On the evening prior to our first homecoming, we had a rally outside the athletic building.

As Denny Duron introduced the starting offense and defense he came to me. I was a walk on. Although I had started every game, I was a new guy. So, it shouldn't surprise me that coach forgot my name. In his embarrassment, he introduced me as "Bubba."

"Bubba?" Now I'm embarrassed. I mean if I cannot be Rod why not Atlas, Titan, Gladiator or Samson? Why Bubba?

Honestly, I was 30 before I started to appreciate all that was done for me in those days. They say the adult male brain is not fully formed until he is 25. Maybe I was slow? But only by reflecting on the perspective of others was I able to see what I was given.

In Coach Duron, I found a man of passion and conviction; a man who loved people, who had a vision for life and a desire to impact the world. He was just that, a great man.

If you want a perfect man you will need to open up the Bible. But if you want great men, men of vision and passion, men who care and equip others, coaches are often the place you will find them.

Thanks for your life, your investment, coach Duron.

Yours truly – Bubba.

Football Formation

Conditioning

"Winning isn't getting ahead of OTHERS. It's getting ahead of YOURSELF."--Roger Staubach, Dallas Cowboys

Conditioning is a big part of preparation. Usually after practice was over, the test was just beginning.

I remember praying that the words "on the line" would not be uttered. I recall those times when I was still hurting from the last game or exhausted from a hard practice, and the whistle would blow and Coach would yell, "On the line."

Running is what you do to reach the end of practice. Running hard is what you do to reach the end of your strength and push it further. Running away is all you think about when your body and mind reach their limits.

Paul Costa was my position coach in college. He was a unique individual, very loyal and very free spirited at the same time. He was like the guy who stood beside you no matter what, and then tell you all the places you were wrong. This "together but separate" lifestyle seemed appealing.

On occasions Paul would yell at me while I was running sprints. "Drury, get over here."

As I approached, his hands would be waving, finger pointing, standing in a posture that revealed how much trouble I was in. Then he would calmly say, even while the finger pointing and hand waving continued, "Just relax, breath deep. Look at me. Don't smile. I'm giving you a little break." While the others ran, I was commanded to rest.

I wondered if Paul gave me these little breaks because he liked me or because he liked messing with the other coaches? Was it about Paul being free to do things his way? Or did Paul want to reward me for my hard work?

It is a nicer memory to think it was all about me. But looking back, it most likely was about him.

Either way it helped me understand that conditioning is about the limits we can endure. And, it is about those times when our minds say "stop" but we press on, doing what is asked of us.

It is hard to feel valued when it feels like you are just being pushed to your limit. While these are valuable moments, we need balance. We need to be called out and praised, or simply given a season of rest, too. Conditioning involves the body, soul and mind.

Maybe you know someone whom you can call away from the rat race and give them a break, someone to inspire with an act of kindness. Don't worry, few of us are too merciful. You might also have opportunity to encourage someone to run harder, too. Remember, however there is a time to run and a time to rest from running.

Football Formation

Fields

"Anyone who's just driven 90 yards against huge men trying to kill them has earned the right to do Jazz hands. " — <u>Craig Ferguson</u>

Football fields, practice fields, corn fields, hay fields--these are some of the fields that have helped me through life. Others have battle fields and fields where they hunted pheasant or deer. What is it about fields?

Back in South Dakota, we had some acreage sowed in alfalfa. And we had an old square bailer. It didn't make square bales, but rectangular bundles of sixty to eighty pounds of eye irritating, skin scratching, flesh puncturing, strength insulting packages of feed. When the temperature was perfect to make you sweat so that the dust and debris clung to you, we headed to the field. We armed ourselves with metal hooks used to grab the far end of the bail, so you could jab the near end into our waists and load. With the bail resting on you, you were now free to turn and stack the bail onto the back of a truck or wagon.

I think the person who developed Cross Fit training must have worked on a farm and had more than one day of clearing a thousand bails out of a field. After the bailing was done, maybe they hauled a hundred buckets of waste from the pens of those hay eaters. For me, a field is a place of both preparation and learning. It's also a place where we need to create and adapt. The hay field prepared me for the practice field.

The practice field is where football players spend most of their time. This practice field refines; it builds our skills. It challenges our character as we test our ability to learn, develop and condition our bodies. The attitude and ability developed on the practice field transfers onto the playing field on game day.

But game day is vastly different. There are no "do overs" or "run it again." Game day has a ticking clock. A opponent and adversaries seeking to keep you from fulfilling your intentions.

On the practice field, the people watching you are looking to help, to assist, to encourage you. On the game field, the onlookers are looking for performance, ability, and accomplishments. The practice field is a learning environment; the game field is a testing environment.

I have found that life has too few practice fields. Once I left college, I had fewer and fewer places where preparation for what I would face included coaches, mentors, and people to help me succeed. It is somewhat strange that we invest so much in the accomplishment of victory on the football field but have so few practice fields for life in general.

I am very thankful for all that I learned on the practice field. I learned to be determined, persistent, focused, and to adapt. I learned to forgive quickly, to not let an offense rule my emotions. And I learned that pain is a part of life. Oh yea, I also learned to keep breathing in times of pressure, confusion, and anxiety.

Not long ago I went back to my Alma Mater. The old field of grass and compacted soil is now a turf field. Bright paint, shining letters, and spongy plastic are now the bed for life lessons and skill development. Things change, but fields will always be a part of our lives to transition us from development to implementation, from practice to execution, from infancy to adulthood.

Gladiator or guppy

*"In football everything is complicated by
the presence of the opposite team."*
— *Jean-Paul Sartre*

In a win/lose world extreme thinking tends to be the only right way to think.

It was the first practice in college when I began to learn extreme thinking. Over a hundred men were crowded on the field seeking to find their places. The grass had yet to be scarred with the sun and the hard feet of men. The lines across the field were crisp and white. What was a playground yesterday became a battleground today.

Football Formation

Benches lined the side, not for seating, but for holding gear. Two water jugs held 10 gallons of Gatorade. A hundred guys, two jugs, five minutes to drink...can you tell what's going to happen next?

Some of the men would just "go with the flow." Others intended to make things flow their way. Some of us were proved in conflict and familiar with the pain of conditioning; others were new to this level of competition. Scars on hands and forearms testified to the veterans. Some wore pads as defense against the impacts. Others had no intention of defending themselves and put on pads to attack.

The most revealing action on the field was making friends, or trying to. Some men were just seeking to get along, to fit in and they felt compelled to build relationships. Others knew building friends then only made it harder to do their job. Friendships would come later. Relationships would develop around position and rank. Gladiators and guppies act different on a battlefield.

We had some violent drills. One was called "kiss your Momma." That is where two players ran into one another at full speed, seeking to run through or over the other player. It's the same kind of game four-year-old boys play in the yard when they ram their trucks head-long into one another, just for the fun of seeing the collision. Both the kid's version and the adult version produce a lot of laughter and a lot of broken parts.

Gladiators knew a time would come when they would hurt their opponent. Guppies hoped to be your friend, so you wouldn't hurt them. But if you bang trucks together long enough, some kids are going to go home crying.

Looking back, what did it do for us? Was it just about violence? Was it a call to overcome fear? Was it about posturing? Was it a necessary time of testing, a time to see who could handle the pressure?

A wise book says that there is a time for everything. "A time for war and a time for peace." I might add, and a time for gladiators and a time for guppies.

Football Formation

Anger and insecurity

Once you LEARN to quit, it becomes a HABIT."--Vince Lombardi

Anger and insecurity were my main motivations in life and in football during my first two years at college. Motivations are the reason we act.

Put a hundred guys together who lacked fully developed frontal lobes of their brain, and you have an environment rich in developing anger and insecurity. Comments, body language, even how you feel about yourself in a given moment all contribute. Top that mixture with competition and comparison and you have a football team.

Football Formation

Insecurity can and often does turn to anger. You can however, use anger as fuel for power. Players and coaches learn how to fill up on anger, so they can dominate. Feeling powerful helps in being powerful on the field.

If you are not a player, you might read this and see it as totally inappropriate. It is not. Learning about anger first hand, through experience, is a necessary task. It does help turn the passive aggressive person into a more honest soul. It helps the angry souls understand themselves.

I played angry until my sophomore year. Some people play angry all their lives. All of us have limits to just how far we can go. But anger has a cost. All fuel does. When I played on anger, I had to allow myself to resist being happy, to resist peace, to resist contentment. To perform at the highest level, I had to be mad. My emotions were my motivation.

Even today, I am mostly negatively motivated. If I can't do something, I try harder. I often feel insecure, but use that insecurity to focus, to persist. Not being able to do something becomes fuel for striving. But anger may be the wrong fuel to burn if you desire to run a long time.

However, brotherhood and love for my team slowly became the dominate force. My motivation based on fear and insecurity decreased as I became a part of the team. Passion and drive began to come from my relationships, from caring about us as a team and commitment to others. I was still selfish, but that was decreasing. Brotherhood was increasing.

I first noticed this transition when the fourth string walk on kicker was shoved on the sideline by an opposing player. Instead of seeing this as his issue, it was now mine. Before I wouldn't allow you to shave me. Now I wasn't going to allow you to shave anyone on my team. Even this guy I didn't' know.

It's funny how football can take an insecure, angry guy and helps him transition to brotherhood, community, loyalty. The guy who cared only about himself can become the guy who watches out for others. Yea, football is like that.

Take an individual and put him on a good team. In time the team will beat the individual out of him and leave behind a better man- a man fit for society. The posture of brotherhood defeats the need for anger and increases our security. Don't fight it. Go with the flow.

"I mean it now"

"You FAIL all of the time. But you aren't a FAILURE until you start blaming someone else"--Bum Phillips, <u>Houston Texans</u>

What kind of world do we live in where we have commentators talking us through twelve hours of playing poker? Is this the result of having 896 TV channels or the result of a society that doesn't do anything but watch?

Regardless, I learned what a "tell" was. And Coach Paul had a tell.

> ***Tell - (especially in poker) an unconscious action that is thought to betray an attempted deception.***

Football Formation

In the film room, we always reviewed the previous week's game play by play. Every position got scored. If you performed well you got a "nice job." If your performance lacked, you got coached. Often, the words to describe your performance were a combination of how the coach was feeling and how you did.

The film room can often sound like a prayer room. "O my God," "for heaven's sake," and other divine expressions reveal that football is played on earth, but God is involved. "What the hell" is an expression that indicates your performance was so bad, both God and the coach agree it was a divine failure.

But Coach Paul also wanted to mess with us. Maybe he got bored and needed something to do or maybe he just liked getting into our heads. Because every now and then his comments were preceded by "I mean it now."

Everyone who knew Coach Paul knew he meant what he said. If you didn't take him seriously, you soon would. He was the kind of coach you wanted to please. He was your best friend and worst enemy all sealed up in a concrete bunker. His picture is in the dictionary next to the word authority.

Over time, we learned that an angry tone of "I mean it" was going to lead into a comment about the impossible being required. It would be a harsh command for a guy to make five blocks, simultaneously. Or it could be a demand for a player to run across the field in a fraction of the time possible and recover a fumble. "I mean it now" was a key to being chided to do the miraculous. If you took responsibility for not doing the impossible, he laughed. If you didn't take responsibility, he said it again.

"I mean it now," meant what is wrong with you that you can't block both those guys at the same time. That is your job. They are running right next to each other. Don't even think someone else is supposed to help you. "I mean it now."

Football Formation

Wind knocked out

"Remember, TOMORROW is promised to no ONE."--Walter Payton

Wrestling, baseball, basketball then football: That was the order of my development in organized sports. The order of the experience probably has a correlation to where you grew up. Wrestling would have always been first for me. I'm a twin, and my mom insisted that we wrestled pre-birth.

Organized football started in seventh grade. The school day started with intermural flag football before school and ended with the junior high practice for those who made the team. If you lived in a rural area, you might be on a 7 or 9-man team. I grew up in Rapid City, big enough for 11-man teams.

Arriving an hour and half before school, I traded my tee shirt and blue jeans for a tee shirt and sweatpants. Next, you tied a belt around your waist and inserted two flags which were to hang where your back pockets go. You made one loop only; there was no wrapping the top of the flag around your belt to help it stay in place.

A referee was in charge of the game. Not some friend. The referee was the official, usually one of the coaches or male science teachers. They had whistles and wore a striped shirt. They ended all arguments, and if you didn't like the call, you were free to head to the gym and get ready for school.

Gone forever were the days when the person owning the ball, or the kid threatening to quit and make the teams lopsided had the ruling advantage. No longer were we subjected to bullies or crybabies. We had come of age, the age of the official.

It was a kickoff. I was running down the field and had my eyes on the guy returning the ball. I never saw how it happened, but it happened. I got hit in the stomach, and the wind was knocked out of me. For the first time, I had that sick to your stomach, breathing but not able to catch your breath thing going on. Like a fish out of water you gasp but nothing seems to come in.

I lay there about a minute, which was long enough for the football coach/referee to see that I was still alive and tell me to either get up and play, or get off the field. I was holding things up. Being raised forty years ago, living in a farm community, and having a religious background, I didn't know I had choices, so I crawled off the field. As soon as I could breathe again, I rejoined my team.

When we played in the yard with our friends, a good injury could get you 5 or 10 minutes of sympathy, especially if a couple of the guys wanted to run home and get a drink or go to the bathroom. But now that I was in Jr. High, the game was not going to be slowed down. OK, they did wait as I crawled off the field, but they also asked me to hurry up.

Another addition to Jr. High was the locker room. The locker room was more than a place to shower and change clothes. It was a place to laugh and re-live the game. The attention that I did not receive on the side of the field was more than repaid in the locker room. It wasn't mean-spirited laughter that sought to put me down while building itself up. It was rather that kind of humor that connects and builds community even in adversity, and celebrates success even in the little defeats.

It has been a long time since I lay on that field gasping for breath. I can still see the coach looking down on me, like some giant talking to an ant. When I tried to hear what he is saying, all I could hear was me gasping for air.

Gasping for air-- in football and in life, we all do that. I hope you have a locker room full of friends with whom you feel free to laugh and share life's moments. A team, like family, gives you a reason to crawl off the field, catch your breath and get back into the game.

Team

*"Today, you've got a DECISION to make.
You're gonna get BETTER or you're gonna
get worse, but you're not gonna stay the
same. Which will it BE?"--Joe Paterno*

I was one of the biggest and fastest kids on our junior high team. I wanted to be a running back. However, sometimes good coaching puts us in our place while at other times it allows us to find our place.

During pre-season, I won the starting half-back position. Surprise: big kids can run fast. The offense had about six running plays: three to each side which included a screen, a quarterback draw, and several passing plays were I stayed in to block. On defense, I played defensive end.

Our first game was a tight contest. We were a grind-it-out team, seeking to run over players more than run around them. The game was low scoring. I ran for my first official touchdown in that game. We won. I don't know for sure what the score was so my memory cannot justify scoring the winning touchdown; however, that touchdown was to be my only one.

The following week I was moved to the line with the other big kids and my twin brother. It had been decided that I could do more for the team in a different position. Someone other than me made the call. I was sad. While I wanted to be a back, I wanted to be on the team more.

Teams value input and require that players take on the responsibilities assign them. In both football and in life, we cannot always be whatever we want to be. Working with other people demands we live within boundaries. It's a form of honor.

My Mom and Dad never asked me if I wanted to move to another town or school district so that I could play in the backfield. This was their community. They cared about everyone's interest, not just ours. Dad never contacted the coach or complained. Working together on the team made us prefer one another. It wasn't always perfect, and politics did entered in. Yet for the most part, we worked it out by living together.

Over the years, I have encountered people who played the game, but were not actually on a team. There were players who saw only themselves. Some were broken souls unable to share life with the team. Some were lonely people who had no vision for community, or team.

Football can help us live life. Life is a team sport composed of people and communities. Sometimes we get what we want, but most of the time, there are compromises. Sometimes we keep the same role our whole life, but more often, our role changes, and more than once. It's not about being a victim or a doormat. It's a welcome mat, a place where life involves a team.

Forty years after the games are done, I see that some guys have a book full of statistics and others have a book full of friends.

Football Formation

Make Sure You Have a Mouthpiece

"Success isn't measured by money or power or social rank. Success is measured by your discipline and inner peace." –Mike Ditka

"We're going to start hitting tomorrow and everyone needs to have a mouthpiece."

Kmart was where I got my first mouthpiece, a "u" shaped semi-flexible piece of plastic. The instructions told us to boil the piece in water and then to insert the mouthpiece into our mouth and bite down. What junior high kid knows how to stick hot plastic in their mouth and bite down?

Football Formation

The next day revealed a variety of attempts. Some kids had the original raw plastic hanging from their facemask. I guess mom or dad thought that it was a better choice than following directions. Some kids had their mouthpiece hanging on a plastic string, a condition caused by overheating the plastic and then dangling it like a tea bag. Bobbing the tea bag (mouthpiece) up and down in the hot water allows the strap to thin out into a thread.

Some kids bit down so hard, there was no plastic left to protect their teeth. It swelled out under their lips and looked like our older brother's chewing "chew".

Only a few kids had the perfectly formed mouth piece. The instructions said nothing about trimming the mouthpiece so that every tooth was protected, and gagging avoided. We knew which kids had dads or older brothers who had played football by the way they managed their mouthpieces.

In life, what we know and don't know isn't always that obvious. In football, everyone who looked at our helmet face saw the level of our skill hanging there. That piece of plastic was a sign saying, "I got lucky," or "I didn't have a clue how to do this." Maybe some revealed the tendency to overheat, or revealed a fear of biting into hot plastic. Mine said, "Burnt gums; will try anything once."

By the second week, most kids who had a deformed or ugly mouthpiece had lost theirs, requiring the purchase and reformation of a new one. I think I got my second one from the sporting goods store. I was hoping it would have better instructions. Instructions are good for most things, even if we don't read them.

I have a favorite instructional saying, "You don't know what you don't know." You might need to ponder that a moment.

Football has a way of revealing what it is we don't know. But it also trains us. It teaches us how to learn, how to move past failures and mistakes and how to try again. Over the next ten years of playing football, I became immersed in the discovery of knowing what I didn't know. Then I would discover new aspects of myself, others and life.

The embarrassing moments of my first mouthpiece are long past but that experience is an enjoyable memory. And that's what life is full of, isn't it? Many of our mistakes can be turned into wisdom over time. What we don't know how to do, we can learn. And once we learn it, we make sure our kids never go to practice with an embarrassing mouthpiece dangling from the facemask.

Don't ever let your first attempt become your identity; keep re-forming.

Chump

*"Self-praise is for losers. Be a winner. Stand
for something. Always have class, and be
humble." –John Madden*

Words, ideas come with feelings attached.

Cowboy country was long gone. Parking lots full of
pickup trucks with a gun rack were replaced with
cars from distant lands. The common greeting of
"howdy" brought laughter. My new outfits from
Kmart, the newest store in town, brought some
chuckles. It wasn't bad. Just enough to make me
feel out of place.

The dorms had a common living area with TVs,
some vending machines and pool tables. As I

walked through this area a young man from the South stared up from his shot and said, "Hey chump." Now I had never heard the word "chump" before. Maybe the sound of it triggered me. Maybe I didn't know chump was southern for howdy. Maybe I was just nerved up and needed something to do to let off steam.

What I do know is that within moments, because of the sound of a word I had never heard before, and some feeling of disrespect, I was ready to fight. I grabbed a teammate, pushed another aside and made my presence known in the most intimidating way I could. At that moment, my life was on aggressive auto-pilot. And all because of the sound of a word I had never heard before. Crazy – right?

I googled the definition of "chump" as I wrote this. Google says it is "a foolish and easily deceived person." Maybe that team mate knew me better than I thought? Looking back my actions seem to define foolish. How many of us have been triggered by the combination of words and feelings?

In football, this can also be true about the snap count, the play call and the motivational phrases we use. Each word is intended to have a feeling leading to an act of the will. On the negative side, words can invoke disrespect, fear, or insecurity. A coach or a player can use a word that evokes a feeling that either motivates the will or causes a person to lose focus or become confused.

Who knew a game of "X's" and "O's" would be so vulnerable to words and ideas?

On the positive side, a team can build a culture using words and ideas that unite and motivate. Taking the time to communicate ideas and attaching the right feelings can help the team have a unified will. A collective determination can be the result of feelings that arise from words like brotherhood, valor, integrity, or never give up.

Every season thousands of men and boys gather together on the football field and hear some words of direction. Words are used to motivate, to inspire. Words are used to unite and develop commitment.

In life, with all the use of different words, it is wise to consider whether our words invoke the feelings we desire.

Football Formation

Facing Defeat

*"The only place success comes before work
is in the dictionary." –Vince Lombardi*

Very few times did I go into a game thinking we were going to be defeated. That particular day, was one of those days.

I had surgery on my right knee and although I did rehab, it was only at about 70%. As a result, I didn't have the quickness and power I once had, especially in the first few steps. My mind was also frequently telling my body stuff that didn't help my confidence, like "This is going to hurt," or "if you make that cut, your knee is going to go out." It seemed as if I had developed an inner voice that was telling me I was defeated before I even started. That voice persuaded my emotions going into this game that I wasn't going to do well.

Consequently, the last two weeks of practice convinced me I wasn't going to do well. While experience and the respect of my team mates allowed me to secure my place on the starting line, in a few moments my experience and respect could mean nothing. What would matter was my performance. The other team knew I had been hurt. My emotions were low in the locker room while across the way some defensive players were up.

The first offensive series were ok. It was mostly straight ahead blocking and no stunts by the defense. The second series involved a screen play, so I had to pull and get downfield. Our team also ran some cross blocks to counter some of the stunts that were starting to take place. No one on our team could perform the Jedi mind control thing, and as I kept thinking about my knee, my limited ability level and getting hurt again, I started to miss some blocks.

"Try something else."

Coming off the field my coach stopped me for a moment and said, "If what your doing isn't working, try something else." That is what I needed to hear. So on the next series of downs, I created a new (for me) technique. Let's call it the flop and roll. Rather than trying to move my opponent out of the way, I sought to hinder them from going to the ball. In the past, my shoulder pads had been the main tool. That day I used my side as I tried to become a section of fence that required the defensive player to either go over or around. It wasn't great, but it worked better than what I was doing before.

I wish I could tell you that I have became a great success at "trying something else." I haven't. I found that most of the time my faithful nature tends to do the same thing over and over. I try harder. I try with more passion. I try with greater focus. I enjoy being creative. But creativity in the face of the daily grind can be a challenge. Do we all tend to do what we have done before? For example, that moment we order at the restaurant. "Let's see, I try the same thing I have tried a thousand times before."

Facing defeat? Learn to try something else.

Football Formation

Laughter and love

"The most valuable player is the one who makes the most players valuable." –Peyton Manning

Smilie Roberts played center on the offensive line. He was from Louisiana, I think. As a Cajun, gumbo, swagger, and half-funny humor were his forte. To me, it seemed like most of his jokes were half-told or miss-told. But we all laughed anyway. Maybe we laughed because his story didn't make sense. Maybe we laughed because he laughed, and we wanted to join in. He was a joy to have on the team.

Every team needs laughter. It relates to love. It's a kind of communication that breaks through the pain of duty and the displeasure of sacrifice. Being able to laugh at one another and with one another is a part of maturity. Being able to make fun of oneself is a sign of security. Allowing others to join in is a sign of humility.

Smilie had such charm that our coach was subject to his ways. When Smilie thought we needed a little rest or when a little humor would lighten up a practice, he made sure that a story or antidote would emerge from under his helmet. Most often Smilie started with "hey coach." Then anything from a "you know what you call a cow with two heads," to a "you know what my grandma used to say," would emerge. Each saying was presented with a smile, a head bob or hand motion matched each phrase.

While football and life are not all fun and games, some of it is. I like men who are comfortable laughing at themselves and with others. Smilie got us through a lot of long days. Maybe every team needs a center like Smilie.

Snot blower.

"There definitely needs to be water on the sidelines for these players, but I also had some Gatorade just in case they were allergic to the water or vice versa."

— John Madden

Both in high school and in college, we had guys on the team who would go over to the drink table, take off their helmet, put a finger on the side of their nose and blow snot all over the drinks. It is a horrible part of my memories. It bothered me.

What kind of guy blows snot all over the drinks? Stupid!

Football Formation

Every time I confronted a snot-blower, I got the same response. "What did I do?"

Really? You are so unaware of your surroundings that you can't see that table full of drinks. You are so self-absorbed that what is happening around you is unknown and unimportant to you?

Forty years later, I know that life is full of snot-blowers. Some people live in a life bubble. They appear to be good people, for the most part. Yet they don't realize that the world they live in is bigger than their own personal space. A good football player knows where your snot is going.

You know what happened, don't you? We ended up drinking snot with our water or Gatorade. Yep, we pretended it wasn't true, but it was. Life doesn't provide the opportunity to replace all the drinks. There are not enough resources in life to replace all the stuff that gets messed up. We learn to live by "making the best of it." We push what we are drinking out of our minds, make sure we are taking our vitamins, and swallow.

If you know how to help a snot-blower please contact me. I still interact with them. They haven't killed me. But boy, O boy, they sure irritate me.

Block

Speed is often confused with insight. When I start running earlier than the others, I appear faster. -Johan Cruyff

Football is a game of mistakes. Whoever makes the fewest mistakes wins. -Johan Cruyff

"Just block."

It was the end of the season in South Dakota and the snow on the field was 6 inches deep. The line had put on plastic gloves to help keep warm - not the normal kind of plastic gloves, but the kind that go up past the elbow, the kind used on the ranch out in the livestock barn- the gloves used to go up the rear end of a cow to "pull" a calf. When it comes to cold weather, you do what you gotta.

With bovine examination gloves on our hands and freezing snow on our feet, we took our positions and pretended to block, pretended because it was a joke. At best, we could stand and push. On a great play, we might get one or two steps before falling to the ground. Wet frozen ground covered by slush is not the foundation for serious football. But the backs saw it differently.

It's one thing to be slopping around in the slush. It's another to have people intentionally grind your face into the muck. Maybe days like this are payback for not thanking your lineman? Maybe days of slush bowls are just a test of endurance? Maybe it's the result of playing football in the fall, in the north?

But regardless of the conditions, the backs want the lineman to block.

Both life and football have times when we are totally distracted and have no intention of becoming un-distracted. We are unable to focus under these circumstances. It's like being told to jog while surfing. We all have limits and standing in six inches of slush on a frozen field, wearing examination gloves was my limit.

That day the linemen got a lot of blame. We were not doing what others wanted us to do. Over the course of the game everyone had the opportunity to chew us out. We just didn't get the job done and for the most part we didn't care. Football was not on our mind. We were thinking about going home; thinking about freezing, slush filled socks and shoes; and thinking about sticking our hands down on the freezing ground over and over again. We were also thinking if we faked an injury, could we get away with it? Is there ever a place to sluff off? And if life and football have no unimportant plays, how do we deal with total distraction and blame?

Relationships, not performance, seemed to be the only redeeming factor. In those moments when I didn't care about my performance, I needed to be challenged to care about others. When our back came into the huddle crying, broken down by how the other team was destroying him, we decided to respond. The ability to overcome our situation was empowered by our care for our friend, our teammate. The fears and tears of our friend gave us a resolve to protect. No longer were the conditions the adversary. The other team was. What we once heard as blame, was now heard as a cry for help. "Just block" went from an accusation to determination.

How many times in life is that true? How often do we hear blame when we should hear a cry for help? No one wants to build a culture of grumbling or complaining. We all have the opportunity to blame others when they are doing the best they can.

However, often in life the only help we have in defeating apathy and despair, is care. Sometimes "just block" means someone is getting hurt.

Frustration

"Football is like life. It requires perseverance, self-denial, hard work, sacrifice, dedication, and respect for authority." —Vince Lombardi

"Home job" is when the officials intentionally give the advantage to the home team. If you play long enough you will experience this. I don't know why it happens. Maybe it's politics. Maybe it's a reaction to a news article. Maybe your coach made the wrong people mad.

It was my second year in college. We were playing an away game. Things were not going well. We threw a number of interceptions in the first quarter. Four, I think.

Football Formation

We also griped, complained, mocked, and insulted the officiating team. We openly challenged their calls. We came into this game expecting to win. But instead we were humiliated. It wasn't that things weren't going our way. Things were being prevented from going our way.

It was late in the fourth quarter. We threw another interception. The back returned the ball up his team's sideline. He was hit and started to stumble to the ground. I speared him.

Spearing is where you use your head and shoulders as a spear, striking the other player as they fall to the ground. It is not a legal blow. You can injure someone. I knew that.

After the impact, as soon as I was off the ground I was punched in the face by the other team's coach. A flurry of kicks and punches impacted me. Two referees came to my rescue and held each of my arms attempting to drag me from the crowd. But what actually happened is their attempt to rescue resulted in assisting the other team. I was helpless to protect myself. After the game, my face was swollen and my legs were covered in abrasions.

My frustration led to theirs. Frustration can be the weather conditions needed to produce a tornado.

You can't control tornados. They just produce destruction until they run out of energy.

Looking back on that day, I see that in the moment of the game I felt justified. But later I saw how a cheap shot trigged a chain of events. I see in retrospect that the lack of the ability to control myself led to a total loss of perspective and a justifying, in the moment, of whatever I did.

I decided I would not be that guy again, and not because of the consequences of the game, but because of the consequences on my soul. I don't want to be a person who injures others because I am frustrated.

Honestly, life offers more opportunity for cheap shots than football ever did. In football, everyone is padded up. In life, few people are. In football people know that impact is a part of the game and that we always need to protect ourselves.

I don't want people to need to protect themselves when they are around me.

Football Formation

Fear

*People who work together will win,
whether it be against complex football
defenses, or the problems of modern
society.*

-Vince Lombardi

There I was: a 240-pound lineman standing on the twenty-yard line, waiting for the kickoff. My job was not to receive the ball, but to be a personal protector for the back who did. As the ball fell from the sky, I moved into a position that allowed me to intercept an opponent running full speed toward the tackle.

Football Formation

Much of the time I had an angle, so the blow was more deflecting than direct. At other times, the contact was head on. And occasionally, two defenders ran side by side seeking a way to tackle the back who was directly behind me as I raced up the field.

Being a personal protector on the kick off allowed me some unique experiences. One of those was having my sinuses drained out my nose through impact. I guess this is where the phrase "getting the snot knocked out of you" came from. It's a funny experience seeing your snot shoot out of your nose and onto the chest of your opponent. Only once were my eyes open when this happened. Most of the time I just saw the remnants of my snot on my facemask and felt the tingle of clean sinuses. But after I saw it once, I knew what was happening.

Another experience was having my helmet break on impact. For me, it wasn't the actual helmet that broke, but the brackets that held the face shield in place. The impact shattered the bracket allowing the mask to crash in on my face, bending inside my helmet and trapping me. We didn't have bolt cutters at the game, so I had to lie on my back on the ground while my coach stood on the helmet and pulled the mask off my face.

Sinus clearing, helmet busting impacts could cause a player to develop fear. Most of the time, the player doesn't have time to consider how much the impact is going to hurt. But when you are the personal protector and have time to consider the impending impact, you find that fear is present. I learned by experience that this is going to hurt. Late in a game, I found myself slowing down so that the impact wasn't so severe. I never knew exactly what was going to happen. But the fear of what might happen was real. How was I going to deal with this?

Fear is not overcome by being stupid. Pretending that fear does not exist or trying to overcome fear by self-deception, didn't work for me. I had to face it head on.

I loved playing football and I loved being in the mix of things. So, love helped me beat fear. I wanted to make the play more than stay away. I overlooked the facts about what might happen and focused on what I wanted to happen. No one was making me play football. I wanted to play and I wanted to play without fear.

Fear may not come from the condition of running full speed into another player. But fear can and does seem to come to all of us from the perception of what we are running into. In life, we often find ourselves running into the unknown, into a pile of bills or into an empty house. We find ourselves facing adversity.

Football helped me learn to deal with fear. Life is full of impacts. We all need a way to overcome and learn to deal with adversities.

Run head on into the conditions, not in the sense of self-destruction, but in the sense of not avoiding our fears. A head on approach is not about getting through the moment. It is about becoming a person who is wiser, and skilled at facing intimidating things.

If you're a mom or dad, sister, or brother you have a personal protection job to do. If you are a coach, leader, business owner or even a bus driver, you have some personal protection assignments to care for someone else. To do those jobs you are going to face some impending impacts that are going to hurt, because they involve risk. You can do it.

Character is the most common tool used to face fear. But we also have times when character is not enough. We may be placed in a position beyond our ability, beyond our character. What should we do? This is where we need someone beyond and outside ourselves to help. We need a coach, instructor, advisor, or Lord to empower us to stay in the game or to take us out, maybe not out of the game, but out of that position.

When we have done all we can do, we need help. It's just the way life is. It's why football is a team sport. One day I did hurt my knee while blocking on a kick return. It was the beginning of the end of my career. But I still enjoy remembering those moments when I left the other linemen at midfield and trotted toward the goal line with backs.

Football Formation

Mindset

"Football is like life - it requires
perseverance, self-denial, hard work,
sacrifice, dedication and respect for
authority."
— *Vince Lombardi Jr.*

Drills are intended to enhance skill but they also create a pecking order.

I got into my stance across from the defensive end. We had run this drill a thousand times. My goal was to block. The defense was to tackle the ball carrier three yards behind me. There was no game to win. It was a drill to improve our ability. But everyone was watching and pride was on the line. Most of the time we faced a player close to our skill level. That allowed everyone to get the most from the drill. But every now and then things got lopsided.

When a second team guard was paired against the leading linebacker we could often see desperation dripping from his helmet. Even though the linemen planned to do his best, he felt defeated before the whistle ever snapped. Football has squads, and we all learn our place, often because someone put us in our place.

I still smile in recalling our practice drill because I remember that second team guard intentionally blocking before the whistle, taking the superior linebacker off guard. The coaches reset the drill, but the offensive player did the same thing again. The third time the guard responded to the Coaches correction by yelling, "Why should I wait for him to kill me?" I admired the rule breaker for taking it to the other guy.

Life sucks when we have negative emotions. When we feel that we have failed before we start, that is depressing. When the outcomes are on public display and our past experiences whisper that we are going to be put in our place, again. Are we just to accept it? Are we to live defeated?

Football players need faith.

Believing is a part of football and a part of living. Coaching involves taking an unbelieving player and turning him into a believer. It's a journey from hopelessness, through perseverance, and finally to commitment and confidence.

Commitment is where even the impossible is something we strive for willingly. Believing we might has led many to success. Basic faith leads to investing in improvement, it drives forward. Commitment motivated by believing may motivate us to stay longer in the weight room or it may cause us to jump the whistle in a drill. Commitment is more than trying harder. It is the "all in" on poker night.

In life and on the practice field, many often see commitment in relation to perceived victory. If the player cannot see himself winning, why try? The joy of striving is thus destroyed. Learning is devalued. Persistence is a pain in the butt if we are not able to get what we want quickly. We have lost faith and begin to think that what is not true today may be true tomorrow.

Be the person who is positive even in negative situations, and not because you pretend the negatives aren't there. Just believe. Have faith to

Football Formation

work hard, keep improving, face giants. And every now and then come off the line early and set the opponent back on his heels. Even if you are penalized, sometimes it's worth it.

Good

Your TALENT determines what you can do. Your MOTIVATION determines how much you are willing to do. Your ATTITUDE determines how well you do it.--Lou Holtz

Coach Phil LaPorta was unique. From the way he greeted you to the way he led, it was different. At first, I didn't know what it was about Phil that made him so different. It was more than his laugh, or his sarcasm. It was deeper than his swagger. Something else impacted me.

The offense and defense were banging heads together. It was the days of "lead with the head." The very thing we are coached NOT to do today. That crisp crack you hear when helmet meets helmet was a trigger for joy. Nothing made coaches happier than hearing the sound of a hit, unless it was seeing the opponent lying on his back.

Coach LaPorta coached the line. One day he put on the pads and gave us a clinic. We were experiencing what happened in the professional world. From the forearm blows to the numbing head slaps, we got the full speed experience. Coach Phil was hands on, practical, and he communicated in a very interactive way.

Coach Phil also helped with the equipment. He worked in the training room. He managed and healed; he equipped and supplied. Coach Phil bruised your body and then put ice on it. He ran you dry and then filled the water jugs to fill you up. I guess he was the kind of guy that does what needed doing.

Coach Phil was the first man who impressed me as a servant. Maybe I had just gotten old enough to value caring for others? Maybe I had just never seen leadership like this before? But people who cared and served were not the kind of people who had ever impressed me. I tended to remember the charismatic leader or the bitter jerk, the extreme guy, but not the friendly, faithful person. I had been influenced by the person with either resolve or visionary. However that is not what inspired me the most about Phil LaPorta.

Phil was a good man.

That was the thought I had: good. Looking back over the practices, the meetings, the sidelines and the games, I pondered what made this man stand out to me. "Good" kept ringing in my ears, not from his head slaps, but from pondering, not pounding.

What was good, what did good mean? So, I did what we all do these days. I Googled it. I looked back to see where the word came from. What did the Greeks and Romans consider good? And since I taught World History in high school a few years, I decided to go a little further back in history. When researching moral words and history, eventually you are going to run into the Bible.

In one ancient worship document, Psalms 145:9, this phrase hit me as to why I connected Phil LaPorta and goodness. The phrase went something like this, "The Lord is good, he takes care of everything he has made."

Phil was the first man I met who enjoyed taking care of others. He was not irritated by bending down and serveing. He did not need a platform. He just lived and gave, doing good everyplace it was needed.

Ok, Phil was not a saint. But he was a Saint; he played for the New Orleans Saints 1974-75. So although he was a Saint he wasn't a saint. You know what I mean. Maybe I saw only the good side of Phil. Maybe I was unaware of his whole nature. But what I saw impacted me. Phil was good. He cared for others.

In life and football, we are going to meet some great men. We are going to be touched by success, vision, motivation, passion, and high levels of skill. We also might be fortunate and be impacted by a good man.

The Huddle.

*"Football combines two of the worst things
in American life. It is violence punctuated
by committee meetings."*
— <u>George F. Will</u>

The meeting place for players in a football game is called the huddle.

I'm bending over to let the sweat fall from my face without running into my eyes. John, the wide receiver, is leaning on me, or maybe we are leaning on each other. Phil is trying to use a piece of tape from his knee pad to stop the bleeding on his arm. Hank is tying his shoe. Benny is quoting numbers which relate to sequences of events, formations, and movements. Don is quietly singing some silly song because he just kicked the other guys butt. The huddle is a combination of a hospital, class room, equipment room and therapy session.

In the 1500s, the word huddle meant "to heap or the crowd together." It also meant "to shelter, to cover." That is just what a huddle does. In the midst of activity, stress, fatigue, and information, there is a place where you can huddle together and find some shelter. It's where you receive the information you need to go forward.

There are numerous postures in a huddle. For example there's a guy who stands upright and listens confidently. There is the guy who is gasping for breath wondering what in the world he is doing there. There is a guy who wants to complain and tell you it wasn't his fault. Then there is someone in charge. He gives the orders so you can get on with the process, so you can make the next move and go forward...and take a step towards winning the game.

I have been in a lot of huddles. The ones I remember the most vividly are the extremes, like the times when there was confidence, a sense of victory, or a sense of well-being. I also recall those gatherings of confusion, filled with grumbling and complaining, people fighting and bickering with one another.

Life is like that, isn't it? We have times when we get together in little shelters, places of reorganization. These moments can serve as times for reflections. However we don't always find what we need to take a step forward. Sometimes our world is in chaos.

Life is harder when the moments we need to regroup are turned into grumbling, complaining, and backbiting.

Football taught me that there are times and places for everything. For example, there will be a time to huddle up in the coach's room or in the film room and discuss things, deal with issues, and even vent. However, the huddle on the field has a far different purpose. That is the time when the players must take the information and do the best they can with the information. It is not a place for grumbling and complaining. It is the time and place where even in your sadness you put on the best face you can, and saddle up your determination to move forward.

On the football field, the huddle is not a place to lean on someone else. It is a place where each player learns to stand on his own. Even though you are on a team, with a group of friends, you must stand on your own. That includes learning to stand when you succeed and when you fail. It is a place where you can take blame without responding. It is a place where you can let the praise fall off your shoulders and retrieve it later. In some ways, the huddle is a very humble place.

It is humble because it is exposed. Everyone can see you there. When you are in a huddle, you feel mostly surrounded by your brothers. But the truth is, people are watching. It is like that in life, too. We have places where we feel strong, where we are with our people. But at the same time, our lives are always being watched. There's always someone gazing at us.

Football taught me how to stand alone, but it also taught me how to stand together. Football taught me to accept both blame and praise. It taught me how to be exposed to the crowds and at the same time be covered by close friends, the brothers I love. I miss the huddle.

Trash Talk

"Coaching is not how much you know. It's how much you can get players to do."

-Bum Phillips

A football squad is made up of men. These men have both talent and character and it is character that makes good men great.

That year we had a great squad. They were teachable. Being coachable was one of their strong suits. And that day they needed that asset.

The opposing team was talented, but it was their mouths, not their physical skills, that were defeating us. My kids simply didn't know how to deal with trash talking. Verbal banter and insulting remarks tended to distract the mind and defeat the soul.

"But coach their talking all this shit," was the response given to missed assignments and lost focus. "Why can't they just play the game."

They were playing the game, just not the game my kids had been prepared for. Running off at the mouth is a winning strategy for some programs. At halftime I needed to deal with it.

Standing before my teachable squad, I expressed a simple solution to our condition. "Talk shit, get hit." Eyes rolled back and forth as they pondered this. Then smiles started to emerge and I could see that a solution to the dilemma had been discovered.

No verbal response was necessary. All trash talk could have a single focused response. In the second half we held our opponent to 7 points and celebrated a 41 – 38 comeback victory. Actions speak louder than words.

What do coaches say at halftime?

Football isn't a contact sport, it's a collision sport. Dancing is a contact sport. -Duffy Daugherty

Halftime is an opportunity to motivate and to impart wisdom and knowledge. It is a break in the game that allows for navigation, re-planning, and even repurposing.

In this game we were being destroyed. Several of the impacts had been very scary. You wondered if your teammate was going to go to the hospital. Our team was smaller, slower, and much less talented. Football has divisions for a reason, and we should not have been playing against this team. This was like the story of David and Goliath, but this David had game film on Goliath and knew what he was getting into.

As we entered the locker room at half-time, many of our coaches were shaking their heads. In their soul, they were deciding if they would just plain lie to us about the situation, or if they would try to encourage us. In the end, they tried both. One of the other offensive linemen told me, "I've been beaten every play." No one had a solution. We were giving it all we had. Most of us headed back onto the field determined to take our beating like men, and we did.

Halftime. I think the most frequent event is an emotional dump followed by the re-evaluation of what it will take to walk back out on that field and maintain a vision of success.

For some, a word of encouragement is the key to getting a fresh vision. To others, it could be information needed in order to obtain their objectives. Still, for others, it is their need to know that there is hope from the brothers that even though they have not been greatly successful, their diligence is still what is needed to strive for victory.

While a coach's words may be inspiring, there is more needed to be able to leave the locker room at halftime with a fresh vision and determination. Football is a team sport. And what the whole team does at halftime is the response that is seen on the field in that second half.

Words at halftime are often controlled and managed well, but body language often reveals a different story. It is body language, this communication from posture, that verifies what coaches say at halftime. If their words and their body express different ideas, it will be evident to everyone in the locker room.

I learned from this that wholeheartedness is an essential part of good communication. There is no use pretending everything is going well when your posture is one of irritation and anger. There is no need to pretend that you are happy when you are not. Good communication is honest, not only in the words that we say, but also in the posture that we manifest.

We may not like honesty, but we respect it. Respect goes a lot further than false praise (saying it is fine when it is not). Respect is a better foundation for establishing a future, for developing commitment. False praise is weak in its substance. Most people know false praise when they hear it. They definitely know it when they see it. Most enter the football battlefield better prepared when they know the game is going to be a true struggle, that hardships and hard knocks are still on the field.

Being authentic is inspiring. Pretending that everything is going to be great when it is not is not authentic. Both in life and in football, we know things are going to be tough. For the most part, we accept that. It does not help anyone to pretend. Inspire us to keep committed to the task, to keep pressing forward, because giving our best is all that we are required to do.

Even if you are not the best at giving great speeches, be one of the best in authentic living. Even if you don't have great words, have a great posture.

No one wants to hear it.

I'd write over and over, I will not throw into coverage.

-Brett Favre

You lost. The game is over.

As you walk across the field to greet the opposing Coach, each step gives time for your emotions to surface. You have made this walk a hundred times. And every time that it comes following a loss, it simply hurts.

Your hand is extended, and your response is to shake it, smile and turn. Even if you can't control your thoughts, you have learned to control your body.

103

Football Formation

Everything is public these days. A hundred people with ears and cell phones will be listening in as you, the Coach, address your team on the field. Moms and dads stand proud of their sons, even those who blew a key play or forgot an assignment. Friends of players pose on the field, taking selfies and sensitive to any negativity toward their people. Coaches whisper to one another about what went wrong. Verbal volcanoes waiting to erupt, but held captive by this public moment. A dozen emotionally broken guys who gave it their all, knew it would be enough. It wasn't.

Meanwhile fifty other players aren't thinking. They just feel. Anger, resentment, disappointment, fatigue and a desire to get off the field control their thoughts. Some are dreaming about a date. Others are longing to ice some pain. A few are thinking about quitting the team; they don't play much and sure don't want to "not play" for a losing team.

Everyone is waiting for the Coach to open his mouth and make them feel better. A player who dropped a ball, who fumbled or made a mental error is also waiting. Some kneel for justice, others for forgiveness.

As a Coach when you open your mouth you are going to say something. Your title, position give you power to influence, to impact. People are looking at you because they look up to you. Do you have words for this moment or is it better not to speak?

The crowd, the circumstances have led you to a place where the best you can do is nothing. If you praise one, judgement well arise and demand you condemn another. If you accept this loss, anger will manifest that you're not more of a fighter. If your fighting spirit emerges, you will be belittled for your lack of mercy. So now what?

Smile. Shake hands and pat backs. Tell a few moms and dads that you really love their kid. Don't stop to talk. Keep moving. As soon as you can, yell out the wisest instructions possible in this moment. A few words that will bring closure and set the course to face what is next. "Get on the bus."

This is a postgame speech every coach should memorize.

Football Formation

Drills, drills, drills.

"You got one guy going boom, one guy going whack, and one guy not getting in the end zone."
— *John Madden*

I'm sitting outside right now. It's nearing the end of July. The days are hot and humid. August is coming—that time of year when we go to football camp and face the adversaries of life called "practice." Practice is working hard when you don't have to, so that when you must, you can do something.

Back in South Dakota some of our football equipment was repurposed cattle equipment. A cattle chute used for ear marking and examinations was cut down and became an iron casket. We used it to drill coming off the ball low. That is not a technique used much today. Let's call this cattle equipment drill "the head banger."

Drills are about the correct way to do something. Repetition reinforces. The skill to accomplish is acquired through drills. Being able to repeat a skill correctly is why we practice. Running through a repurposed cattle shoot was not about looking funny. It was about learning the correct way to do something.

In the 70s hitting an iron bar in the head banger could result in a broken helmet. A clang rang out when someone shot off the ball at full speed and raised up prematurely. No one needed to tell the player he got too high. He knew it. Early in the season several clangs rang out hourly. By week four, you seldom heard one. It was like sticking your hand in a fire. You learned by experience.

Later when I went back home to S.D. I noticed the cattle chute was gone. Nothing lasts forever. But I'm sure it didn't wear out. Someone decided to repurpose that material in another direction. Maybe it was cut down again and used to ear mark and examine sheep. I hope so.

However, that old head banger helped me learn the power of drills. It drove into my head the need for constant reminders of poor performances. It gave me a place to learn skills. It was a place of boundaries. It was a place that measured my performance. It was a place used to prepare for game day.

If you keep getting your head knocked, find a place to drill, even if you need to repurpose something, do it.

Football Formation

On the line.

"Ability is what you're capable of doing.
Motivation determines what you do.
Attitude determines how well you do it."
— *Lou Holtz*

Conditioning.

After the fourth wind sprint, I had to quit thinking. It was too exhausting to both run and think. My mind would not let my body rest. "When have we run enough? When are we in good enough condition? How do we prepare for the unknowable? Am I getting in shape physically or mentally? Why learn to control myself when I'm tired? Why in the world would I do this to myself?"

Football Formation

I developed a switch I now call "total authority." When I flipped this switch, I went from independent to dependent. I gave total authority of my life to another, to the coach blowing the conditioning whistle. I didn't argue. I didn't complain or reason. I just obeyed.

Coach never asked me to do this. I just did it. I found it was the easiest way for me to focus on conditioning. All I had to do was obey. I didn't need to decide to run each sprint. I didn't need to convince myself to keep going. I avoided the inner turmoil between my desire to run and my desire to rest. My mind was at peace and I was able to focus on obeying. I could work hard without trying to convince my soul. Coach oversaw my soul. I'm sure you can see both the blessing and the danger in this.

Conditioning is the process whereby we developed into being a better athlete than we could be on our own. That is why we hire trainers, educators, and ministers. It is a basic understanding that we can do more with the help of others, a help that pushes, disciplines, and demands.

And yes, there is a dangerous side of trusting others. We all know stories that have not ended well. But we should not neglect good things just because someone has abused it. There is a time to stand up for ourselves. But if we are under good leadership it is time to obey. It is time for us to be under authority.

One day you will have authority. Being under authority can help you lead with wisdom. Life is a mixture of both being in and being under. This happens on the field, in marriage, in raising kids, and in the market place. We give people authority and in so doing place ourselves under their rule. This is not always a bad thing. In fact, it is a normal part of life. If we don't learn both how to lead and how to be led, life will be very hard.

Football made me more than I wanted to be on my own.

Football Formation

It itches.

Life is TEN percent what happens to you,
and NINETY percent how you respond to it.
– Lou Holtz

When a football player stands scratching his crotch, he may be irritating, but he also might be itching.

Itching is what Frank did. Mom didn't go to college with Frank, so he had to figure out how to wash clothes. Discovering just how many times you can wear a pair of underwear before they have a life of their own may be a part of the college experience. For Frank, the rash was a sign he had not figured everything out yet.

Football Formation

Males, aged 14-18 are the most likely group to have jock itch. Google is full of helpful information. Many of us should heed the wisdom on Google and take care of ourselves. Hygiene matters. Not just for those around us, but for us, personally. Developing a fungus on our bodies is not something we should laugh at, but I am sure if the guys in the locker room see it, there's going to be some laughter.

Some guys didn't shower after practice. I suppose they were too shy. Avoiding the shower in your dorm room, can be costly. I know we all have different levels of hygiene practice. We have people who spend hours on themselves. And we have people who don't spend a moment. Football can provide an itchy reminder that we need to keep our body clean. Your problem today may be our problem tomorrow.

The twin brother of jock itch, is athlete's foot. This brother is highly contagious. It can be transmitted in a gym or shower. This becomes a team issue. And that's the point. Taking care of ourselves properly is also about the team.

Being too lazy or too tired to clean and dry yourself isn't just about you. We all might have to deal with your stuff just like we deal with your stuff on the field and in the bus. Life is a community endeavor and it is necessary for everyone to practice good hygiene because good hygiene, or lack of it, affects the whole team.

Who would ever have imagined that a football coach would need to teach his players how to shower? But if he doesn't, he might end up in an itchy situation.

Football Formation

Rainy days and Sundays.

"The problem with winter sports is that -- follow me closely here -- they generally take place in winter."
— *Dave Barry*

"There is no substitute for work."

--Vince Lombardi

I shared a three foot by four-foot tub of ice with five other guys. Picture a stainless-steel tub about three feet tall, surrounded by half-dressed men. An ankle, two knees, a wrist and some poor guy with his face next to another guy's butt is trying to soak his elbow in the ice. Everyone in this little circle loves football, enjoys practice, and is tired of pain. We all want a day off.

Football Formation

Working harder and doing more is the common default for improving. I believe this is mostly true. But late in the season your mind, body and soul just want some time to rest. I know a lot has changed since the days I played (1970s). We hit Tuesday through Thursday, while running drills at full impact throughout the season. It's not that way anymore.

The size and power of players have changed over the years. Kids these days begin lifting weights in middle school and the use of supplements can turn a 145 pound want a be into a 175-pound impact wrench. Even as equipment has advanced, so has the ability of the players to impact with force. Football is a physical game and requires time to rest today.

A football season is like running a marathon with a time limit. You must complete the course but within the amount of time you have. Every hour counts, let alone every day. The season is a balancing act between rest and practice. Do we make the most of every opportunity or do we make every moment an opportunity?

I recall standing on the field on a rainy day. Mostly I remember fanaticizing about being anywhere else. It was prior to lightning warnings and rules, so we all stood on the field waiting for our coaching staff to make the call. I think a thousand prayers reached heaven from the field that day. Prayers to get us out of the storm and into the film room. But on this day, no prayers were answered.

If practice was ever canceled it was like a mini-Christmas. It was a gift. Not sticking your head into a sweat infested plastic bubble, not filling your mouth with a dirty piece of plastic (called a mouth piece), not banging your body into the guy next to you was a delight. Sitting in shorts in a film room was a retreat. There you were watching, no one hitting you, no one shoving his hand in your face, no one driving his forearm into your chest. If you had an icepack, you popped a hole in one end and sipped ice water.

Sundays was our only day of rest. Unless of course we needed to come in for ice or therapy. Rainy days and Sundays. OK, extremely rainy days and Sundays are days of rest and maybe answers to prayer.

Football Formation

Doesn't fit.

"When it's too hard for them it's just right for us!"
— *Marv Levy*

I remember receivers going to the equipment room on picture day. After pictures, they traded in most of their over seized pads for smaller ones that didn't hinder running and catching. Looking as big as the other guys and being able to function in the game was different and required different pads. Presentation and function are not the same. One receiver got pads so big that he looked like a slice of pizza. But the maroon and gold uniform helped this image and with the slightest imagination his numbers could be seen as pepperoni and sausage. Decades later he confessed this was a stupid thing to do.

How the equipment fits is a big deal. In junior high, when the kid put on his helmet and could spin it around, that was hilarious. In high school, it was humorous, in college it was sad. In my day pads were made of plastic. Today, they may be Kevlar and some space age foam. I don't know. Maybe I'll ask my son. But regardless of how well they are made, if they don't fit, they are no good.

In Jr. high, Peter was a receiver. He was a seventy-pound bolt of lightning. Both his size and his speed made it hard for the pads to "hang onto him." Shoulder pads have a plastic shield that covers the area where your shoulder transitions to your arm. This shield is on a hinge so that when you raise your arm, it lifts up, allowing you to raise your hand over your head. Both Peter's jersey and his pads were too big so the shield got stuck in the up position and blinded his vision, not once, but a thousand times. Sometimes even Peter's head was sandwiched between these protruding pads producing something close to blinders on race horses. Receivers should not wear blinders.

How many of us have been impacted by incorrectly fitted equipment? I know my first shoulder pads were way too big. We were lined up across the gym floor from biggest to smallest. The equipment was handed out in descending order. When they got to me, I got the next size pads. It was then my job to fit into the pads, not the job of the pads to fit me.

I recall the sound of us running sprints. It was like a wind chime of plastic. When we ran onto the field for games, we rattled. That is funny now, but then we were all serious. Today, it might be seen as some hilarious YouTube video. But back then, it was boys fitted for battle. Just not fitted too well.

I also recall one college game where I had "running back" knee pads in my pants. I was an offensive lineman. My pads were usually about half an inch thick. Whether by design or by re-engineering, the pads I had that day were about a quarter of an inch thick. I guess it made for easier knee movement. I sure felt like I could run faster. But I also felt it while I was crawling on the field with some defensive lineman on my shoulder.

During my second year in college, I got a new helmet that had just come on the market. It was an air, water combination. The cells in the padding of the helmet were a combination of water and air. After one hard impact on a kickoff, I felt the water running down the back of my neck. The water pack in the helmet had burst. I learned that new is not always better. And I learned that "better" is the result of fixing what is new.

A while back I visited a pregame locker room. The players were taking selfies. After applying some black out under the eye or twisting the helmet to give some gangster look, they shot selfies. Shoulder pads were made to look several inches bigger than waist size. One guy was scratching up his helmet to produce a few war scares before snapping out his image.

Do we dress for protection or presentation?

Look good if you can, but protect what needs protecting. That is a good lesson in life. It is not a posture of fear, but an act of wisdom. Try to envision what needs to be cared for, and care for it. Complain if the uniform and equipment don't fit. You may not get better stuff, but sticking up for yourself is one way to care.

Over-excitement.

Pro football is like nuclear warfare. There are no winners, only survivors. - Frank Gifford

Randy was a great guy who was full of nervous energy. As he stood and banged his head against the concrete wall before each game, he was just getting ready. And there was Kevin. Kevin was sitting on the training table getting his ankle wrapped for the third time. The first two just never felt right. And even though Kevin didn't start, his pregame energy required everything to be perfect. I would tell you about Bill, but it is too irritating to recall. This guy's nervous energy drove him to talk endlessly. Never-ending words flowed from an anxious heart producing meaningless noise. Energy and emotion are the fuse of self-destruction in the person without self-control.

When our emotions have control of us we lose our ability to control ourselves. We find ourselves doing stupid stuff.

Randy is back at the wall. Coach just told him he is to receive the kickoff to start the second half. Bang goes the head. Crack goes the helmet. Fear slashes across Randy's face. Should he tell the coach what he just did or play with a cracked helmet?

Practical jokes.

"In order to win the game, you must first not lose it."

--Chuck Noll

Guys can be stupid. Stuff does get out of hand. People do get hurt. And practical jokes are a part of life. Often, it's the way a little guy makes a big impression, or how the person who is overlooked gets seen. Most of the time, though it is just for laughs.

Atomic Balm was a hyper *Bengay*. So if you took that cream and rubbed it into the jock of a "friend," you played a joke on him. And hopefully, you did not destroy his chances at having a family.

Football Formation

The only thing worse was "the waffle." To waffle someone, you took a tennis racket and a hair brush. With the tennis racket over the naked butt of your "friend" you vigorously scrubbed their butt with the brush. Once the tennis racket was removed you saw why this was called "the waffle."

There is a story about a judge who had to rule on a pornography case. The lawyers wanted the judge to give a description of what pornography was so that they could prepare their case. The judge refused to give a description saying, "I'll know it when I see it." Practical jokes are like that. We often don't know if we have gone too far until we see it. We might not always foresee consequences, but we can avoid repeating our mistakes.

Spitting.

"The man who complains about the way the ball BOUNCES is likely the one who DROPPED it." – Lou Holtz

Growing up in South Dakota involved spitting. Chew was common. We joked, "don't date a girl that chews." But chewing isn't the only reason people spit. We spit sunflower seeds and bugs out of our mouths. We spit out stuff clinging in our throat and stuff we didn't want to swallow.

In my world spitting is Ok. The concern is, where does the spit land.

I've been in the huddle and have the wide receiver behind me spit on my back. I've experienced the

Football Formation

quarter back spit in my face like some passionate preacher. I've had the defensive lineman spit on my hand, seeing if I would move and get an "off sides" call.

Just the other day I was parked on Grand View Drive, a scenic drive along the river in our area lined with parks and picnic tables. As I read my book, I sucked some snot out of my sinuses and spit out the window on my car and anointed the walker next to me with some undesired blessing.

I'm not sure but I think the words "I'm sorry" comes from the Latin, "Oops, I spit on you." Few people feel better with an apology. Most want the stuff cleaned off.

Severe injuries.

"It's not the size of the dog in the fight, but the size of the fight in the dog". – Archie Griffin, <u>Cincinnati Bengals</u>

"The harder you work, the harder it is to surrender"--Marv Levy, <u>Buffalo Bills</u>

Unfortunately, injuries are a part of football. Some of those injuries are severe.

I can still see the play when a 145-pound high school safety was run over by a 215-pound back. Mitch was fearless and attacked the back without reserve. Knowing he needed to engage the tackle low, he did. But the back also lowered his head and ended up catching Mitch's neck with his shoulder pads. Mitch ended up on his knees. Then the impact bent Mitch over backwards. The scream was far softer than it should have been as both his knees were folded back to the ground. Football was over for Mitch.

An honest look at how football forms us requires an honest look at injuries, even serious injuries. There are 500,000 injuries each year in football.

I am sure my knee and hip replacements are, in part, due to my football years. While in the hospital getting my new parts, I visited with people that never played football, but were also having joints replaced. I didn't know exactly what would result from choices I made in the 70s. But if I compare the wear and tear on my body to the lifelong benefits football has had on my life, I would choose football again.

I lost contact with Mitch. He might have wanted to make a different decision. There are life choices that I would re-do, just not football.

I don't want to deal with the choice to play football, but consider how we deal with injury. From my experience with a knee injury, I look at life with a different perspective. For the most part, my life had been pain free. I had a world view more inclined toward invincible than vulnerable. My injury opened my eyes to the world of being sidelined.

I had to take the sideline in the third or fourth game of my senior year. My knee had too much slop in it and the tape job was not able to support a quick maneuver. The off-season provided rehab. But I should have finished rehab and started the season late. The path I choose resulted in dropping out of the season early.

A football season is short. Once it starts there is a limited window to achieve victory. I feel this is a huge factor in how we dealt with injuries and how people dealt with us. From the moment of my injury I was moved away from the team and toward the trainer. My place was given to another. The focus of the coaches and players did not include me. This was offensive. I had given so much, but after getting hirt I was overlooked.

That was not harsh, only practical. I felt a desire to be a part, to be involved. I didn't understand how my injury changed my situation, not only for me but for the team.

Through my seasons in football, I lost many friends to injury. I cared about them but continued to focus on the season. Now I began experiencing what they experienced. Sidelined.

Sidelined is a good word for it. The Sideline is where you keep the stuff. It is the staging area for the game. It is the place for close observation but limited participation. My value dropped. I wasn't a player anymore.

Last year I went hunting with my brothers. I had had a knee replacement just a few months prior. We had a great time, but walking was limited for me. They cared for me, watched out for me. But I was limited. I could not experience what they experienced. Injuries don't break relationships but they do limit and change them. They change what we share.

My football injury helped me understand what others experience. It gave me a revelation on how people feel when they cannot join in. It made me understand how being left out is more than a lack of wanting to join in.

There is a saying: "No pain, no gain." What do you gain from the pain of a severe injury? Compassion. Compassion should be for both those on the sideline and those striving to finish the season. Success sometimes comes through obtaining compassion.

I'm a football coach

"Leadership is a matter of having people look at you and gain confidence. If you're in control, they're in control." –Tom Landry

"I wish I was a football coach." Five men all nodded in confirmation. The sixth shook his head no. He was a coach.

People tend to see the status. They see what seems to be a powerful and influential person, leading a united team, celebrating life through playing a game. Onlookers, seeking a sense of victory, adventure, or brotherhood may see the coaching staff as captains—leaders who are conquering the world.

Football Formation

But being a football coach is a lot like pastoring a church, overseeing a correctional institution, and working in the public relations office of a despised politician all at the same time. It is a life that is wonderful and exhausting and a job where you are only as good as your last game and where people feel it is their duty to tell you what you are doing wrong.

You lead high energy young men whose brains are not yet fully formed, but their opinions and desires are. These men have parents with opinions and desires, men who have friends with opinions and desires. In fact, football is a lot like church. No matter how good it is, there is always a "but." But what about that kickoff, dropped punt, that third down in the fourth quarter when you passed the ball but should have handed it off to my Tommy who was ready to score. Do you even know what you are doing?

What am I doing? Am I winning or losing? Am I building men or maintaining a program? Am I baby-sitting or longing to be home with my own family? And who am I trying to keep happy? The school, the other coaches, my players, the fans? "Man, this job has a lot of pressure!"

Pressure. It is the third pot of coffee consumed in the office. It is pile of papers on the desk hide the plans for travel, meals, and hotel. It is another pile containing the updates to the playbook along with the desired squads for certain situations. Yet another pile contains medical reports and contacts for recruiting. And yesterday's lunch tries to hide the list of people who want you to call them back: players, parents, officials, and administrators all in need of communication. Someone in the office cries out, "here are some changes we need to make this week." You send your family a text and make another pot of coffee.

When a player or coach explains what they do—football: a majority of people become excited for them. They love the thrill of the game and are avid fans of specific teams. They feel a sense of ownership because they cheer for their team and participate as a spectator. Little do they know the amount of effort it takes to run a program.

However, remember that you get to stand with people who sacrifice together, who physically overcome, who face fears and endure pain together, all to achieve a common cause. You get to see boys become men and men become noble. You get to enjoy victory, hear praise, laugh in the face of pain, and enjoy the achievement of the impossible. You get to coach football. It might be the best job anyone could ever hate.

What makes a man, a man?

"Success isn't measured by money or power or social rank. Success is measured by your discipline and inner peace." –Mike Ditka

What makes a man, a man?

Some players step away from high school and onto the college campus with confidence. Some players pretend to be confident. For most it is a mixture of both.

Randy was a star running back in high school. He was well known, often the center of attention at events. People loved to come up to him and hang out. Randy accepted his identity in this role, but with college his life was about to change.

The first day Randy arrived at university, it was all so different. No one knew him. The coach that recruited him was inviting, but also inviting to the other twelve kids he recruited too. Randy stood in an intersection of identity. What path would he choose?

This is a pivotal moment. Either pathway leads to an unknown future. The path on the right leads to connection with new authorities, developing a new support system, discovering new friends and working out a new life.

The path on the left was the path of seeking to remain the same and have all the circumstances and situations around you change. It was the pathway of resistance and insecurity.

When the choices are exposed, it seems like most people would choose to change, to grow. But to many work hard at staying the same and have everything else around them change. Often it takes a life impacting moment to redirect them. Football is often that very moment.

Attraction

Kelly Drury

Gentlemen, it is better to have died as a small boy than to fumble this football. - John Heisman

Football attracts people and attraction is a key component of football's process. It is a tool used by coaches to recruit players. It is how the wide receiver obtains his quarterback's attention by a wave of his hand. It is also what the coach uses when he stands silently in the film room. Football also provides other attractions that directly affect my life.

When you are attracted to a football player you soon realize that you do not get just the one player; you are involved with the whole team aka the family. I met my husband during his college football days. I pointed him out in the cafeteria and stated, "I'll take that one!" He felt the same way and actively pursued me showing up in my dorm where he had never stepped foot before.

I soon began to realize in our early dating, that there was a brotherhood established, and it took time for me to be "let in." The coaches also had curfews, accountability, and discussions of distractibility when it came to dating. Todd was my focus, but the football team was his family. Even with that, I was still attracted to him and the family unit. I wanted to be a part of it.

When I was accepted into that family, the whole team was there. Our family dinners, friendships, mentors, etc. What it looks like now and before was/is a lifelong blessing of personal relationships and friendship. The special moments we have together are remembered by our football family. The football family helps us capture a thousand snapshots of adventure and joy.

Football attracts people, but its attraction doesn't stop there.

Gifted

Kelly Drury

"When you're GOOD at something, you'll tell everyone. When you're GREAT at something, they'll tell you."--Walter Payton, Chicago Bears

How many gifted people make up a team?

From the donors who support the team, to the administrators in the office; from the educators, to the training staff; from the parent who believed in him, to the recruiter who discovered him, which gifted person do we want to leave out?

Todd discovered his gift through football. Now he wants to be a good football coach, but he wants to be great at leading men. That's his gift.

Football Formation

Gifts are given to help others. From the running back gifted at breaking tackles, to the offensive coordinator gifted at picking apart defensives, our gifts are given in the context of helping others.

Every August, Todd steps onto the field excited about sharing his gifts. His title may be coach, but his gift is the "molder of men."

If you don't know your gift, you might be focusing on what you can obtain. Change your focus. What can you give? What are you great at giving? In what way can you help others?

I once heard that a wise man gives away so that more can come to him. Be a river not a dam.

Through football, my husband uses his gift— coaching young men. Just as his coach guided him four years ago, Todd guides others. Fast forward another eight years. It's August. We hit the field excited about the new year and molding young men in football and in life.

I wonder if anyone who stands on the field today will be coaching tomorrow?

Plato

"The ONLY discipline that lasts, is SELF discipline"--Bum Phillips

I'm sitting at my son's desk. Scattered across the top are several napkins, some scrap paper and a few notepad pages. Each one is filled with football doodles. "X's" and "O's" and lines and boxes all communicate an idea. Offensive and defensive coordinators are like Plato. They ponder and imagine. They look not only into a matter but beyond it. They are in quest of an idea that will change reality on game day.

Plato believed an idea was more real than reality. He felt the idea of something was more real than the thing itself in this dimension. The idea of a perfect play would be more real than a well-executed play in the game.

OK, before you throw this book across the room because you wanted to read about football and not philosophy, let me share the point. Great ideas lead to great reality.

It is late in the season and rumor has it that the defensive end who I am blocking has already committed to go professional. This hybrid between a leopard and a bear has dominated the division. His appearance is impressive. His ability even more so. But my Coach has an *idea.*

On every play of our opening drive I am to miss the block and as quickly as I can, double back and blind side him. All three of our opening plays are sweeps left so I have the chance to take an inside route and hopefully swing back into the backfield and catch him in pursuit. It worked.

The idea, when implemented, created a hesitancy in a great player. All game he kept looking over his shoulder wondering if someone was going to blind side him. Every chance we had, we did.

Napkins need players and players need napkins. We need both ideas and execution. Every coach should read Plato and "The Art of War."

Deception

*"We would ACCOMPLISH many more
things if we did not think of them as
IMPOSSIBLE."--Vince Lombardi*

In my mind, I was a lean mean playing machine. But that guy in the video was plump, not that flexible, and more like a bowling ball. The man in my mind and the man in the game film were not the same guy. But they were.

I recently heard a man say, "The ability to break free of deception requires that you trust others more than you trust yourself." Football demonstrates that truth. In my mind, I was playing a great game. Or at practice I was giving my all, doing exactly what the coach asked. I saw myself using the right technique or having the desired posture.

Film brought to light a truth greater than my perception. Often a play that I thought was totally blown, wasn't that bad. And plays that I thought would earn me a "that a boy" ended in embarrassment. The film was my reality check.

During practice, the coach was the reality check. Without the use of an iPad, or even a cell phone camera, you need to trust your coach to make corrections. Today coaches can show a player. Back when I played we had to be able to listen and trust. Even though your mind said you were doing it right, it was only right after the final approval of another.

Our drop back pass protection technique was intended to form a "U" around the quarterback. The center was required to stop his opponent or drive him to the side. The guards and tackles tried to get their opponent to go around, or if they crossed over toward the center, to drive them to the other side.

As your opponent approached, you had to make impact, then use your hands and legs to create separation. You didn't want the defense to get a hold of you or to stay in physical contact with you.

Separation allowed you to make another impact, each one slowing down the rush and hopefully turning your opponent to the outside.

Some linemen had a hard time getting that. They thought they were hitting and creating separation, but everyone watching saw a different story. At times, we thought we pushed the opponent wide around the quarterback only to discover we were tripping over him directly behind us. What we thought was a violent blow overpowering the opponent was seen by others as a simple head-bump.

The world is full of deception. The videos that should offer truth are edited or neglected. The idea of a reality other than my own perception is rejected. In football players often come to the field with little life skill at being teachable. More time can be spent on proving stuff than developing skill. Even after watching a video of himself, a player can say, "I don't believe I did that."

Trust is needed for truth. Reality is another word for truth. In the real world of football, you need to trust or you will end up in deception. You will end up living a life that is not true, not real. It may seem harmless. We all fantasize about how great or how bad we are. But when we're not daydreaming, it is best to live in the real world, and that world requires trust.

I can recall a day in August during two-a-days. It is a 90-degree day with 90 percent humidity. The sweat was running down my face and burning my eyes. My helmet felt like it weighed 14 pounds. My pads plugged the air from flowing through my pants and jersey. I felt like I was wearing plastic wrap. And of course, it was the day that coach told us we were skipping the water break so we could get off the field sooner, yet I had no idea what sooner meant.

Then the coach yelled at me. Drury! In my mind, I was working hard. I was focused. I was ….

Trust. Why did I need to trust his opinion? Why did he have authority to tell me how hard I was trying? Why was his perception more important than my own?

In the future it might not be long before satellites video our every moment, but until that time, we need to trust someone to avoid deception. It is not that enjoyable to watch those old game videos. I would like it if they revealed a leaner, more agile me, but the truth is, that is not who I am.

Football Formation

Orange

"The GREATEST mistake is to continue to PRACTICE a mistake"--Bobby Bowden, Florida State

The first three possessions when we got the ball were three and out. Our total offensive was less than twenty yards, but that time we were driving the ball. When we were on our own 32-yard line we had a third and eight, but a quick slant was successful and built our confidence. Then on their 40-yard line we ran a draw and got to the 18-yard line.

It was now third and four on the 12-yard line. Everyone knew we were going to punch it in. We lined up and had a play called to the right side.

Football Formation

Our quarterback came to the line and saw the defense stacked to the right with additional players in the box. So, he called "orange".

Orange was our key word to flip the play. It was our audible to take the same play we planned to run, but run it in the opposite direction. The "O" in orange is the "O" for opposite.

With confidence Lenny the quarterback called our "orange, orange, orange" to his left. Then making sure the right side heard the audible, he called off the same to the right. Then, "hike" and off we go. Both our guards pulled to lead the play, but in opposite directions. They collided with each other and we are thrown for a loss. It is fourth down and the drive is over.

"What was that?" Greeted us on the sideline. Lenny told coach the play call. Everyone heard the audible. Who blew the play? The left guard should not have pulled. The play was intended to go the other way. When asked why, he said, "I got confused by all the "orange" calls. I couldn't keep up. Which was the play—was it going right, then left, then right again?"

There was only one audible. The system is not dependent upon how many times you say the word, it is dependent upon everyone hearing the word. Repetition is for clarity, not confusion.

Coach never thought he needed to clarify. He never thought someone would think we flipped the play each time the word was called. In life and football, what we think is inconceivable, happens. What we feel is apparent, is often confusing. One man stood on the sideline and wonders "how could anyone think that way." Another stood and ponders, "how could anyone NOT think that way?"

Repeating yourself may only reinforce what they don't know.

Football Formation

Thank God for coaches.

Football is an incredible game.
Sometimes it's so incredible, it's
unbelievable. -Tom Landry

In many ways, life is like a highway. Sometimes we are the driver. At other times we feel more like a passenger. But we are all on a road, a journey, an adventure. A coach is like a driver's Ed teacher. And he is like a stranger standing at an intersection. You know, the people we ask for directions and help.

But a coach doesn't just point in the direction they should go. They walk down the path alongside you. Some players make the journey easy, others take a much more difficult road. Funny how we are all affected by those who walk with us. Life is much more personal than impersonal, allowing us to adjust our step and pace according to the one walking next to us. And football coaches take some walks with their players, like: walks to administration and to the court house. Walks to the cafeteria and the chiropractors. Walks down the aisle for a wedding or through the parlor for a funeral.

Some pathways lead to a better future. Some manifest impatience. Both are a part of the season we call football.

Looking from the outside you might think that the coaches are all about the team as a whole and winning. Don't get me wrong—some are, but most are about the individual players and guiding them through a portion of life. No one plays football forever, but they will forever be men.

Thank God for coaches.

Drury

Football Formation

Other Titles by Redneck Mystic Media

On Sale on Amazon
(eBook and print)

Jesus and Baseball

Growing in Gratitude

How to Pray

Young Theologians Workbook
      The Lord's Prayer Edition
      The book of Acts 1

Rodney's Author's Page

https://goo.gl/HvzTC1

Football Formation